CONOR
MCGREGOR

Conor McGregor vs. Dustin Poirier

CONOR MCGREGOR

ODYSSEYS

MICHAEL ALLEN

CREATIVE EDUCATION · CREATIVE PAPERBACKS

Published by Creative Education and Creative Paperbacks
P.O. Box 227, Mankato, Minnesota 56002
Creative Education and Creative Paperbacks
are imprints of The Creative Company
www.thecreativecompany.us

Copyright © 2025 Creative Education, Creative Paperbacks
International copyright reserved in all countries.
No part of this book may be reproduced in any form
without written permission from the publisher.

Design by Graham Morgan
Art direction by Tom Morgan
Edited by Kremena Spengler

Images by Associated Press/Gregory Payan, cover; Getty Images/Brandon Magnus, 12, 19, 42, 46, Chris Unger, 4-5, 70-71, Christian Petersen, 8, 11, 59, 75, Diamond Images, 31, Ethan Miller, 51, Jeff Bottari, 2, 39, 64, Josh Hedges, 26, 34-35, Mike Stobe, 52, Steve Marcus, 48; Pexels/Pavel Danilyuk, 28; Shutterstock/antoniodiaz, 24, Leeloona, 60; Unsplash/aboodi vesakaran, 6, Matteo Grando, 14, Sylwester Walczak, 56; Wikimedia Commons/Andrius Petrucenia, 40, Ebyabe, 63, Miami Beach Police Department, 66, ocean yamaha, 20, Pak Roman Yurievich, 69

Library of Congress Cataloging-in-Publication Data
Names: Allen, Michael (Children's literature), author.
Title: Conor McGregor / by Michael Allen.
Description: Mankato, Minnesota : Creative Education and Creative Paperbacks, [2025] | Series: Odysseys in extreme sports | ATOS 6.4 | Includes bibliographical references and index. | Audience: Ages 12-15 years | Audience: Grades 7-9 | Summary: "Step into the Octagon with mixed martial arts (MMA) fighter Conor McGregor. Witness triumphs, challenges, and risks in this extreme sports title for high school readers. Includes action photos, a glossary, index, and further resources"- Provided by publisher.
Identifiers: LCCN 2024025236 (print) | LCCN 2024025237 (ebook) | ISBN 9798889893134 (lib. bdg.) | ISBN 9781682776797 (paperback) | ISBN 9798889894247 (ebook)
Subjects: LCSH: McGregor, Conor, 1988-Juvenile literature. | Mixed martial arts-Ireland-Biography-Juvenile literature. | Ultimate Fighting Championship (Organization)-Juvenile literature.
Classification: LCC GV1113.M34 A45 2025 (print) | LCC GV1113.M34 (ebook) | DDC 796.81092 [B]-dc23/eng/20240719
LC record available at https://lccn.loc.gov/2024025236
LC ebook record available at https://lccn.loc.gov/2024025237

Printed in China

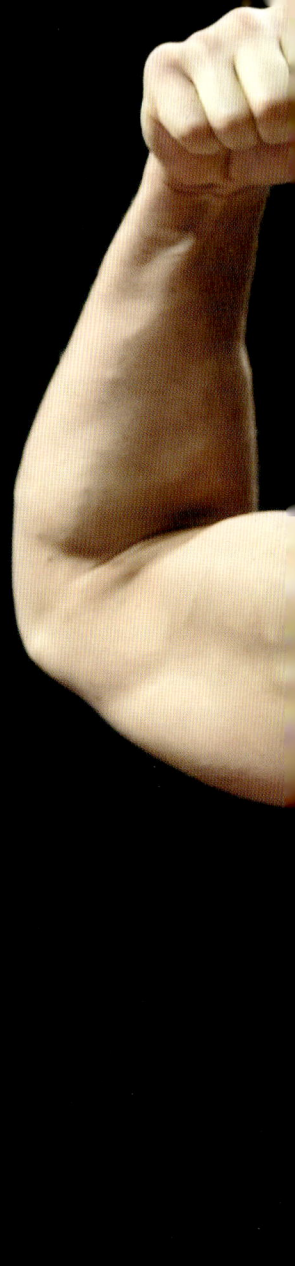

Conor McGregor poses on the scale during the UFC 246 weigh-in.

Introduction

Conor McGregor finally got his wish. No Irishman had ever come this far in mixed martial arts (MMA) fighting. It only took 13 seconds for him to win the Ultimate Fighting Championship (UFC) **featherweight** title from champion José Aldo on December 12, 2015, at the MGM Grand Garden Arena in Las Vegas, Nevada.

OPPOSITE: Conor McGregor after his victory over José Aldo in the featherweight championship fight at UFC 194 on December 12, 2015, in Las Vegas, Nevada

In the opening seconds of the first round, McGregor threw a left hand but missed. Aldo lunged forward with his own left, but McGregor had a second left waiting and ready. That brutal punch knocked the 29-year-old champion to the mat. McGregor knelt down and pounded Aldo twice more in the head. Referee John McCarthy quickly ended the fight. The 27-year-old Irishman's dream came true. "Again, nobody can take that left-hand shot," McGregor recalled at the time.

McGregor's left hand has taken him around the world, along with his southpaw and orthodox stances. McGregor has won most of his victories with knockout punches or technical knockouts (TKOs). In addition to his fighting skills, McGregor is famous for his tattoos: a tiger on his abdomen, gorilla on his chest, winged crucifix on his neck, thorns on his spine, and writing on his left forearm.

McGregor hits Aldo with his second left.

OPPOSITE Conor McGregor before he faces Khabib Nurmagomedov in the lightweight championship fight at UFC 229 on October 6, 2018, in Las Vegas, Nevada

How did McGregor win both the featherweight and lightweight titles? It's fair to say he did not have an easy climb to the top of the UFC. No one from Ireland had ever done it, he had no role model, and even his parents didn't think he could succeed. But McGregor persevered, and luck was on his side. The UFC was expanding to Europe just as he was rising up the ranks. Once McGregor got to the top of the UFC, he dominated the sport. He even fought his childhood hero, a world-famous boxing champion. McGregor experienced wins, losses, and highs and lows. What does his future hold? To find out, let's see where he came from.

CONOR MCGREGOR

Childhood: From Soccer to Boxing to MMA

McGregor was born in Dublin, Ireland, on July 14, 1988, to Tony and Margaret McGregor. He was raised in Crumlin, a working-class neighborhood of Dublin. Tony recalled his son's birth to the *Irish Independent*: "His fists were clenched coming out of the womb so he was ready to fight. The midwife said, 'This fella is going to be a boxer.' It was an easy birth as Margaret was only in labor for an hour, so Conor was in a hurry to make himself known."

OPPOSITE: A view of Dublin, the capital of Ireland and Conor McGregor's hometown

McGregor went to Gaelscoil Scoil Mológa school where he played soccer. He got bullied at school, so he decided to learn how to box to defend himself. He joined the Crumlin Boxing Club from age 11 to 17. However, his mother, Margaret, didn't like the idea of her son switching from soccer to boxing for fear of him getting hurt. Tony recalled that his young son was not the trash-talker he would later become. According to Tony, his son's outrageous persona developed with age, which Tony found very entertaining.

Phil Sutcliffe, who coached McGregor at the Crumlin Boxing Club, recalled to *Boxing News* that the future MMA superstar trained very hard and wasn't the type of boxer who needed to be pushed. Sutcliffe noted that McGregor was becoming a good boxer and winning bouts, but decided to quit boxing "when he was 15 or 16" for

MMA fighting, which was growing in popularity with young people. Sutcliffe was not a fan of MMA fighting because he felt it was "animalistic," but he could not sway McGregor away from it.

McGregor's dad Tony also noticed his son's interest shift from boxing to MMA fighting, which involved "all the different disciplines" such as martial arts, while boxing was just "one discipline." At about this time, McGregor and his family moved to a larger house in Lucan, a Dublin suburb. McGregor was in his teens.

It was a difficult move for the future superstar who had to leave his friends.

McGregor started going to a new school, Coláiste Cois Life, where he became friends with future MMA fighter Tom Egan. Egan told the *Bleacher Report* that McGregor was lazy in those days and trying to find his identity. McGregor seemed to find the answers he was looking for at Egan's house, where the two young men watched videos of UFC fights and tried to imitate the fighters' moves.

Tom Egan

Plumber's Apprentice

McGregor's dad, Tony, encouraged his son to learn a trade, so McGregor reluctantly became a plumber's apprentice. Some days he worked for 12 hours in plumbing before going to the gym to train. McGregor recalled how much he hated plumbing: "I did not see anyone that was in any kind of healthy shape. I saw that maybe if I walked away from plumbing, I could train two times a day. I could really focus on my diet..." McGregor decided to quit plumbing, but he would have to tell his parents. He had a heated argument with his dad, which almost turned into a fight.

McGregor and Egan started working with trainer John Kavanagh at the Straight Blast Gym in Dublin. Kavanagh, who was nicknamed the "Godfather of Irish MMA," noticed Egan's and McGregor's raw talent, which needed some fine-tuning. McGregor once beat up two fighters in Kavanagh's gym during a sparring session that got out of control. Kavanagh stopped McGregor by pinning and punching him until he promised to train the right way and not engage in street brawling.

McGregor told the *Bleacher Report* that his parents were skeptical of their son fighting for a living. They would ask him what other Irish men had become successful MMA fighters, and he didn't have an answer for them. Without a role model, McGregor would have to find his own way and blaze his own trail. The family arguments spurred McGregor to follow his big dreams.

"You'll be sorry when I'm a millionaire," McGregor told his dad. "I remember saying at 25 years of age I will be a self-made millionaire. And my father laughed at me. And you know, I was a year late... But I did it. I told him so."

McGregor actually became a millionaire many times over. In 2021, *Forbes* named him the highest paid athlete, with an astonishing income of $180 million, of which $158 million was made outside the Octagon. McGregor first made the *Forbes* top 10

"I REMEMBER SAYING AT 25 YEARS OF AGE I WILL BE A SELF-MADE MILLIONAIRE. AND MY FATHER LAUGHED AT ME."

list in 2018, when he was ranked number four with $99 million. He made endorsement deals with Anheuser-Busch, Rolls Royce, Monster Energy, and Bud Light, notes *Sporting News*.

What McGregor's parents didn't realize in the early days was that their son's timing was perfect. He was joining a popular U.S. sport just as it was spreading across Europe. However, it was hard for his parents to see him get knocked around in the Octagon as he climbed the MMA ladder of success.

Blowing Up the MMA and UFC

McGregor's father, Tony, told the *Irish Independent* that he worried about his son's early fights because his opponents were so big. However, over time, Tony realized that his son trained to get the same type of body as the men whom he fought. McGregor had his first professional MMA fight on March 9, 2008, as a lightweight in the Cage Warriors, a promotion based in London. He defeated Gary Morris with a second-round TKO. After that quick brawl, Kavanagh scheduled McGregor for another fight in the Cage of Truth 3 on June 28, 2008.

OPPOSITE: MMA fighters often try to hold their rivals down and throw punches at them during a fight.

Conor McGregor gets confident during a UFC weigh-in on August 16, 2013.

During the weigh-in on the day before the match, McGregor engaged in the trash talking that would make him famous. He told his opponent, Artemij Sitenkov, that he'd knock him out in the first round. McGregor took it one step further and mocked Sitenkov's coach: "You can get it too, old man!" However, McGregor's trash-talking backfired. Sitenkov quickly took McGregor down in just 69 seconds. To make matters worse, McGregor's entire family had come for the first time to see him fight. After losing in front of them, McGregor left the sport ashamed.

McGregor started missing his training days and spent time on his parents' couch instead of at the gym. While McGregor took time off, his buddy Egan was winning in the 175-pound division on the Irish MMA circuit. Egan was starting to live out McGregor's dream. When Egan fought at UFC 93 in Dublin in June 2009, he was the

Rags to Riches

After his first fight, McGregor described his rags-to-riches story during a post-fight news conference: "Just last week I was collecting the social welfare. I was in there saying to them, 'I don't know what's going to happen. I'm signed to the UFC. I don't know. Blah, blah, blah.' Now I suppose I'm just going to have to tell them [expletive] off." UFC President Dana White was impressed with McGregor's first UFC fight: "Let me put it this way: I'm blown away. First of all, it's his first fight ever in the UFC. He walked out tonight and got into the Octagon like it was his 100th fight in the UFC..."

first Irish-born fighter to compete in the big leagues of MMA. Egan's success encouraged McGregor to get off the couch. Ironically, it was McGregor's mother who asked Kavanagh to give her son a second chance in the sport she despised.

McGregor's return to training paid off as he racked up win after win. As a result, McGregor became cockier and more defiant. In 2011, McGregor was insulting other fighters on Irish message boards under the username "The Notorious," a nickname that would stick with him throughout his career. In his next match, McGregor defeated Connor Dillon in a featherweight fight but then lost a lightweight fight to Joseph Duffy. McGregor had a 4–2 record but turned his career around with an eight-fight winning streak in 2011 and 2012. McGregor won the Cage Warriors featherweight championship and the lightweight championship. This was the first time a European MMA fighter won titles in two divisions at the same time.

McGregor's wins started attracting the attention of UFC President Dana White, who signed him

to a contract in February 2013. McGregor cashed his last unemployment check and used it to travel to Stockholm, Sweden, for his first UFC fight on April 6, 2013. He scored a TKO over Marcus Brimage in the first round in just 67 seconds. For that one fight, McGregor made $16,000—and another $60,000 for "knockout of the night." This was a staggering sum of money for a young

Dana White

man who was just scraping by a week earlier on government welfare checks. It seemed as if a giant door had opened. The former plumber's apprentice had crossed the line into the UFC, pocketing more cash than he could ever dream of by fixing pipes.

McGregor was scheduled to fight Andy Ogle at UFC Fight Night 26 on August 17, 2013, in Boston, Massachusetts. However, Ogle had to cancel because of an injury, so he was replaced by Max Holloway. McGregor defeated Holloway with unanimous decision by the judges but tore his **anterior cruciate ligament (ACL)**. This was a serious injury. Surgery and rehabilitation of his knee would keep McGregor out of fighting for almost a year. This was a setback that could have sidelined McGregor permanently, but he put hard work into rehabilitating his injured knee.

McGregor was back in the ring on July 19, 2014, to face Cole Miller at UFC Fight Night 46 in Dublin, but Miller dropped out because of a thumb injury. A Brazilian fighter, Diego Brandão, replaced Miller. The fight was stopped at 4:05 in the first round (4 minutes, 5 seconds into the round), giving McGregor another win and his first "Performance of the Night" award.

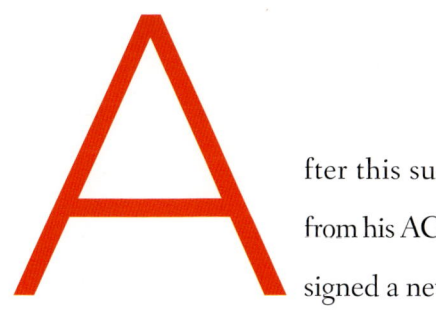After this successful comeback from his ACL injury, McGregor signed a new contract with the

Conor McGregor punches Marcus Brimage in a featherweight fight on April 6, 2013, in Stockholm, Sweden.

UFC. He fought Dustin Poirier at the MGM Grand Garden Arena in Las Vegas at UFC 178 on September 24, 2014. Referee Herb Dean ended the brawl in the first round, after McGregor slammed a left hook behind Poirier's ear and followed up with four hard lefts. McGregor won his second straight "Performance of the Night" award, which brought him a $50,000 bonus.

The year 2015 would prove to be huge for McGregor. He began the year by defeating Dennis Siver via TKO in the second round at UFC Fight Night 59 on January 18,

"MCGREGOR'S RECORD WAS NOW 16-2, AND HIS BIG OPPORTUNITY WAS JUST AROUND THE CORNER."

2015, in Boston. McGregor won his third "Performance of the Night" award for the fight.

McGregor's record was now 16–2, and his big opportunity was just around the corner. On January 30, 2015, the UFC announced that he would fight José Aldo for the UFC featherweight title. The fight would be on July 11 at UFC 189 at the MGM Grand Garden Arena in Las Vegas. To promote the fight, McGregor and Aldo went on a press tour in eight cities across five countries. The press tour ended in Dublin, where McGregor grabbed Aldo's championship belt and screamed at Aldo, who tried to get the belt back. White separated them and calmed the chaos, but he was smiling the whole time. He knew the UFC's biggest fight of the year was on its way.

Before the big fight, however, Aldo suffered a rib fracture and dropped out. During an appearance on ESPN, White announced the news: "Chad Mendes now will fight Conor McGregor for the interim belt." Some

McGregor vs. Poirier

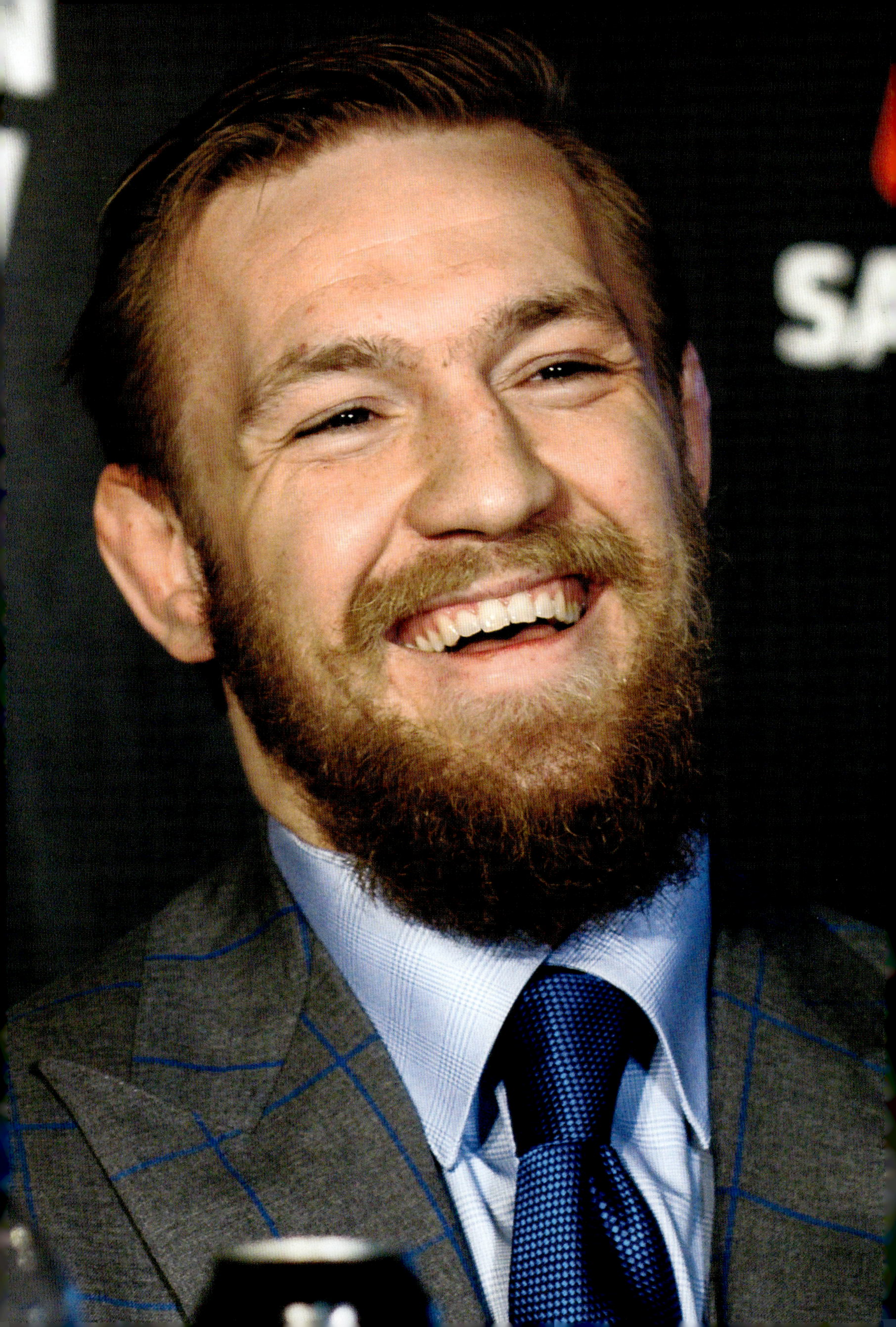

OPPOSITE Conor McGregor promotes UFC 189 on March 30, 2015, in London.

observers were concerned that McGregor would not be able to handle Mendes, a two-time National Collegiate Athletics Association (NCAA) Division One all-American wrestler. But McGregor had been training with Sergey Pikulskiy who had wrestled for seven years with Moldova's national team, reported *The 42*.

McGregor defeated Mendes in a second-round TKO for the interim featherweight championship at UFC 189 in front of 16,019 people. The **pay-per-view (PPV)** brawl set a record $7.2 million profit for an MMA event. McGregor would go on to beat Aldo in December, winning the UFC featherweight title in a record 13 seconds at UFC 194 in Las Vegas. He was an MMA superstar, but could he keep it going?

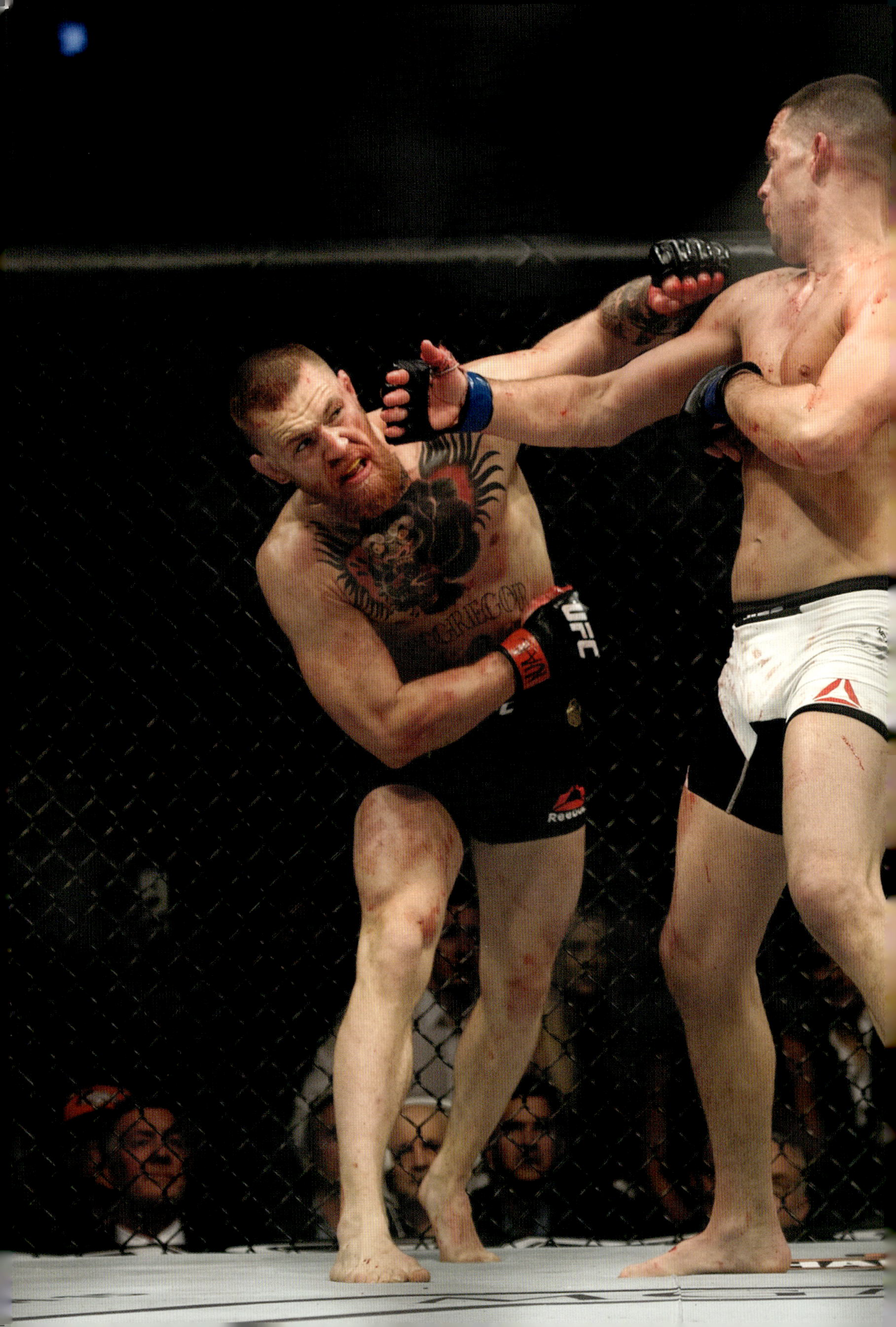
UFC

CONOR MCGREGOR

Defeat, Retirement, Comeback, Mayweather

The year 2016 would be a rough year for McGregor, as he suffered his first UFC defeat. Lightweight champion Rafael dos Anjos pulled out of their planned March fight because of an injury. McGregor jumped a weight class to fight Nate Diaz at UFC 196 in a **welterweight** fight. This would prove to be a big mistake for McGregor.

OPPOSITE: Conor McGregor (left) takes a punch from Nate Diaz (right) in the welterweight fight at UFC 196 on March 5, 2016, in Las Vegas, Nevada.

McGregor and Diaz got physical during a press conference on March 3. Diaz put his fists up in a fighter's pose, and McGregor responded by hitting one of Diaz's hands. The men had to be separated.

Their memorable fight happened on March 5 inside the MGM Grand Garden Arena in Las Vegas. In the first round, McGregor missed a kick, and Diaz shoved him against the fence with an **underhook**. McGregor escaped but took a hard jab from Diaz. McGregor came back with a left, but Diaz unloaded several jabs.

"THE FIGHT WAS NOT GOING THE WAY MCGREGOR'S PREVIOUS BATTLES HAD GONE. SOMETHING WAS WRONG."

McGregor slammed Diaz with a right **uppercut**, and his left-handed shots hit the right side of Diaz's face, which bled from the right eye. Somehow, the injured Diaz was still able to hit McGregor with jabs.

In the second round, McGregor jabbed and kicked Diaz's thigh, and caught him with another uppercut. McGregor pulled down Diaz's head for a knee slam, but Diaz hit him with a right hook. McGregor jabbed Diaz several times, but a hard left from Diaz slowed McGregor down. Diaz used a combination of punches, including an underhook, that pushed McGregor against

McGregor is forced to submit.

the fence. Diaz held McGregor on the fence and hit him with a dozen lefts. McGregor struck back with a couple of left punches, but Diaz slugged him back. The fight was not going the way McGregor's previous battles had gone. Something was wrong.

McGregor went for a **takedown** but got caught in a **guillotine** by Diaz. McGregor escaped but rolled on to his belly, which left him wide open for Diaz to catch him in a rear choke. McGregor **tapped out** in a massive upset.

McGregor vs. Nate Diaz at UFC 202

The fight ended McGregor's 15-match winning streak. He had suffered a huge defeat, and things were about to get worse. McGregor was scheduled for a rematch with Diaz on July 9 at UFC 200, but the UFC announced on April 19 that McGregor had been pulled from UFC 200 because he refused to do a press conference to promote the fight.

"Obviously, we still have a good relationship with Conor," White said at the time. "I respect Conor as a fighter, and I like him as a person. But you can't decide not to show up to these things. You have to do it." McGregor responded on Twitter by saying that he "decided to retire young," while his coach, Kavanagh, added, "[It] was fun while it lasted." Was McGregor serious? Was he going to end the career he had fought so hard to build? Or was he just upset that White had pulled him out of UFC 200?

It turned out to be a short retirement. His rematch with Diaz was rescheduled for August 20 at UFC 202 in Las Vegas. McGregor got off to a fast start in the fight, but then Diaz took control. Would this be a repeat of their first fight? McGregor came back strong in the fourth round, to win with a majority decision by the judges. The fight set the record as the biggest pay-per-view in UFC history, with 1,650,000 tuning in. McGregor was back on top, but challengers were nipping at his heels.

On September 27, the UFC announced McGregor would fight Eddie Alvarez for the UFC lightweight championship in November at UFC 205 at Madison Square Garden in New York City. True to form, McGregor trash-talked Alvarez before the fight: "Show up, take your [expletive] whooping, and

Matching Up to Mayweather

McGregor's childhood friend Tom Egan once recalled that he was hanging out with the 19-year-old McGregor in a bookstore, and the future UFC champ was mesmerized by a picture of boxer Floyd Mayweather on the cover of *The Ring* magazine. "Wow," McGregor told Egan. "Look at him. He is the face of boxing. He's on top of the world." Egan recalled trying to get McGregor out of the bookstore, but he wouldn't go. Egan said McGregor "was visualizing himself in that position—on the cover."

McGregor knocks out Alvarez.

I'll see you later." True to his word, McGregor knocked Alvarez down several times in the first round and used a combination of punches to defeat him via TKO in the second round.

It was the first time a fighter simultaneously had won the UFC's lightweight and featherweight championships. The win also earned McGregor "Performance of the Night." It seemed like McGregor had made a successful comeback and made UFC history, but an unexpected turn was just around the corner. The UFC announced on November 26 that McGregor voluntarily gave up the featherweight title because he had not defended his title enough times in that division. The featherweight championship was given to Aldo.

However, McGregor's coach, Kavanagh, said McGregor had not actually given up the featherweight title.

He said McGregor had been stripped of the featherweight championship by the UFC. "Conor has only been 11 months since he won that title," Kavanagh stated. "There have been many, many examples of fighters waiting 15 months, 18 months before defending it. He's [had it] 11 months, and they stripped him of it. I thought it was very shortsighted by the UFC how they went about doing it."

McGregor, who was still the lightweight champion, announced in November 2016 that he would take some time off to wait for the birth of his child, who was born on May 5, 2017. McGregor also wanted more money to fight because of the sale of UFC's parent company to Endeavor, then known as William Morris Endeavor, for $4.025 billion in July 2016.

McGregor switched gears in the early months of 2017. MMA bouts were not his priority anymore. He wanted something bigger: a boxing match against legendary boxer Floyd Mayweather, his childhood idol. McGregor pushed for the fight on social media and during public appearances. It was finally announced on June 14 that a boxing match between McGregor and Mayweather would happen at the T-Mobile Arena in Las Vegas on August 26.

During a press conference in Los Angeles, California, in July, McGregor taunted Mayweather, an African American, to a point that many felt crossed the line. He

The rules of boxing differ greatly from those of MMA.

wore a suit decorated with the F-word and yelled, "Dance for me, boy!" while Mayweather did some shadow boxing. To many observers, McGregor's "boy" taunt sounded racist. McGregor then changed his taunt to: "Dance for me, sir. Dance for me!"

However, it only got worse as Mayweather and McGregor exchanged profane insults. To many, McGregor looked like a racist. He had to change his image fast. McGregor tried to tone down his racist image by saying of African Americans: "I'm a big fan of the culture." But the trash-talking continued as McGregor's fighting buddy Lobov bragged that McGregor was "better than Mayweather. He is going to dominate him, 100 percent. Believe it." However, former boxing champion Mike Tyson predicted just the opposite: "McGregor is going to get killed boxing."

Mayweather had an undefeated professional record of 50–0. He had beaten some of the greatest boxers: Canelo Álvarez, Oscar De La Hoya, Manny Pacquiao, and others. Mayweather had won championships in five weight divisions. Just like McGregor, Mayweather was an expert at promoting himself and his fights. His nickname was "Money."

In contrast, McGregor hadn't boxed since he was a teen. In preparation for the fight, he trained to box for only 21 days in Dublin, then brought his team to Las Vegas to help him train for just a few days. Would it be enough to win?

It wasn't. Mayweather defeated McGregor with a TKO in the 10th round. McGregor threw a combination of early punches. However, as the fight went on, his lack of boxing experience showed. By the 10th round,

McGregor vs. Mayweather

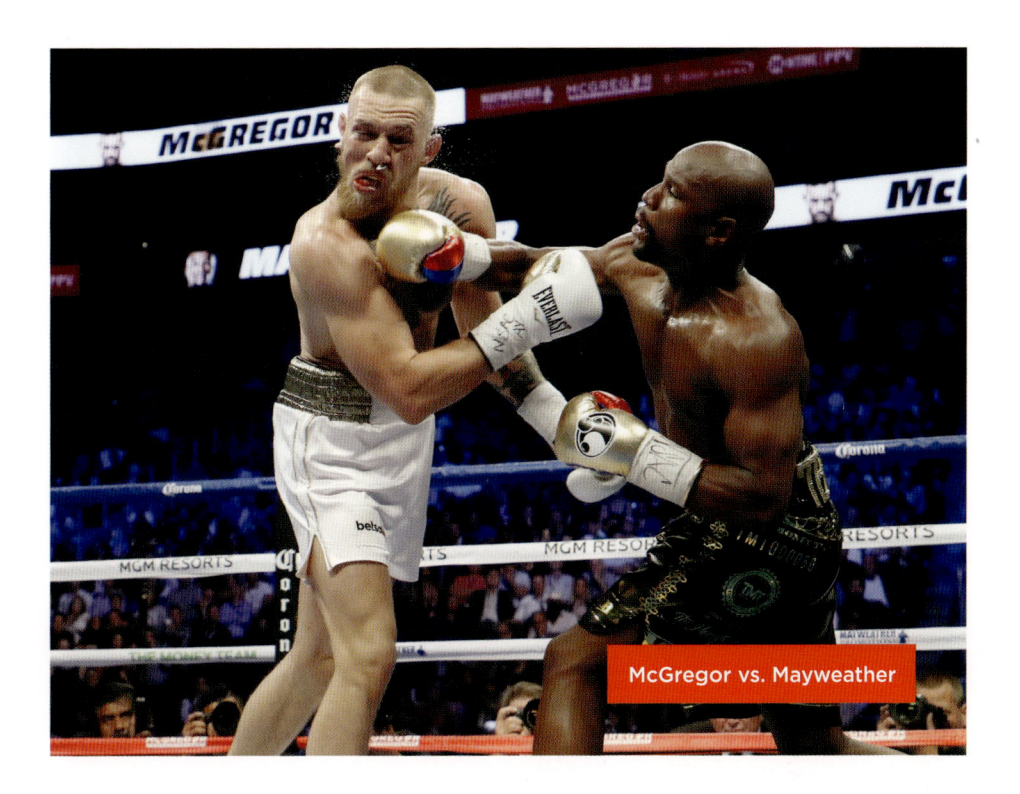

McGregor was leaning on the ropes to stand, which caused referee Robert Byrd to stop the fight in favor of Mayweather. The fight was a massive loss for McGregor, who had claimed he was going to make more than $100 million for the bout.

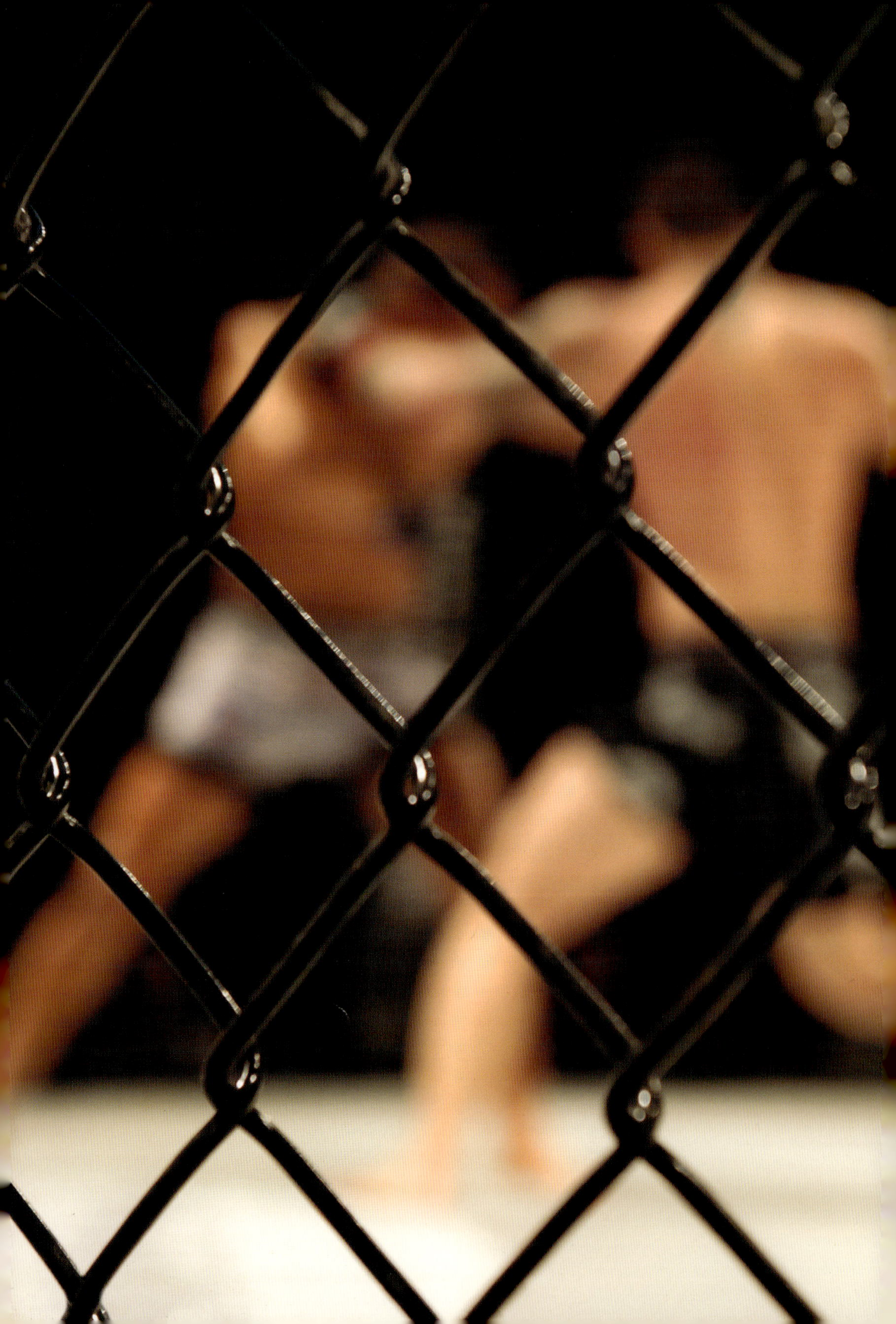

CONOR MCGREGOR

Arrests, Retirement, Comeback, Future Plans

After the 2017 disaster with Mayweather, things got worse. White announced during the UFC 223 post-fight press conference on April 8, 2018, that McGregor had been stripped of the UFC lightweight championship due to inactivity. Undefeated Russian fighter Khabib Nurmagomedov was named the new lightweight champion.

OPPOSITE: McGregor was stripped of his lightweight title in 2018, for failing to defend it.

This happened only days after McGregor was arrested for allegedly throwing a hand truck through the window of a bus carrying Nurmagomedov and other fighters at Barclays Center in New York City. Fighters Michael Chiesa and Ray Borg were injured by some broken glass.

After turning himself into the police, McGregor was charged with "felony criminal mischief and misdemeanor counts of assault, attempted assault, menacing, and reckless endangerment." McGregor got a plea deal that required him to take anger management classes instead of jail time. White claimed McGregor tried to justify his behavior in a text to him. McGregor said he was trying to protect his teammate Lobov, who was allegedly confronted by Nurmagomedov at a hotel.

White didn't buy it. He called McGregor's actions the "most despicable thing in UFC history." But White

'Made Whole'

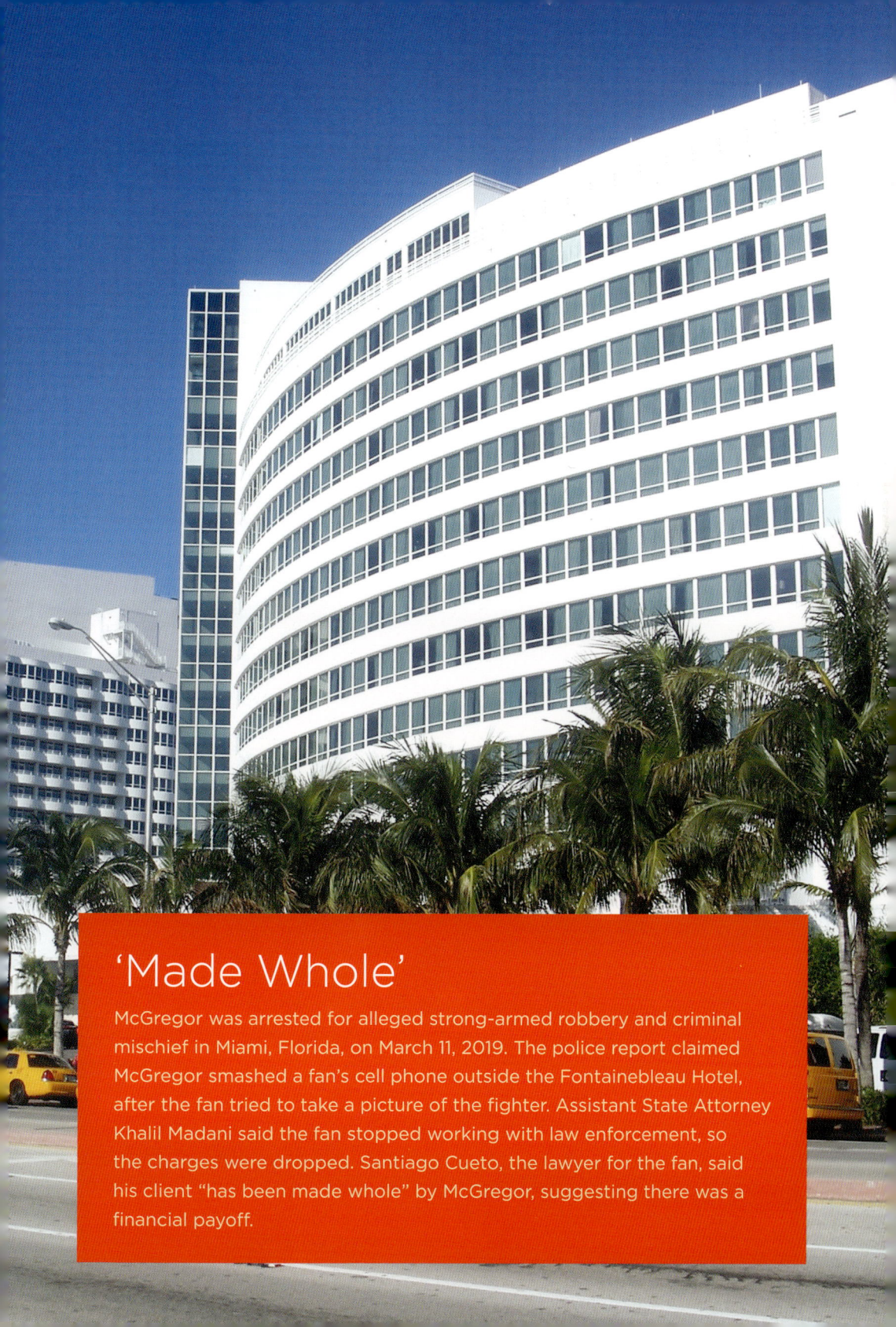

McGregor was arrested for alleged strong-armed robbery and criminal mischief in Miami, Florida, on March 11, 2019. The police report claimed McGregor smashed a fan's cell phone outside the Fontainebleau Hotel, after the fan tried to take a picture of the fighter. Assistant State Attorney Khalil Madani said the fan stopped working with law enforcement, so the charges were dropped. Santiago Cueto, the lawyer for the fan, said his client "has been made whole" by McGregor, suggesting there was a financial payoff.

Nurmagomedov attempts to submit McGregor.

wasn't that upset. He used video of the attack to promote a fight between McGregor and Nurmagomedov for the UFC lightweight championship at UFC 229 on October 6 in Las Vegas. The pre-fight publicity was huge as McGregor would be fighting to get his title back. However, it was not to be. Nurmagomedov defeated McGregor with a **rear naked choke** in the fourth round at the T-Mobile Arena. After the match was over, the fighters' teams got into a post-match brawl. Police and security guards had to break up that fight. McGregor announced his retirement (again) on social media on March 25, 2019.

However, White claimed on CNN the Irish fighter would return: "Conor McGregor will fight again... Conor likes to be in a position where he holds the cards, and he does what he wants to do. And, you know, he and I figure out how to work together and how to make it all happen."

McGregor's mugshot after his arrest in Miami

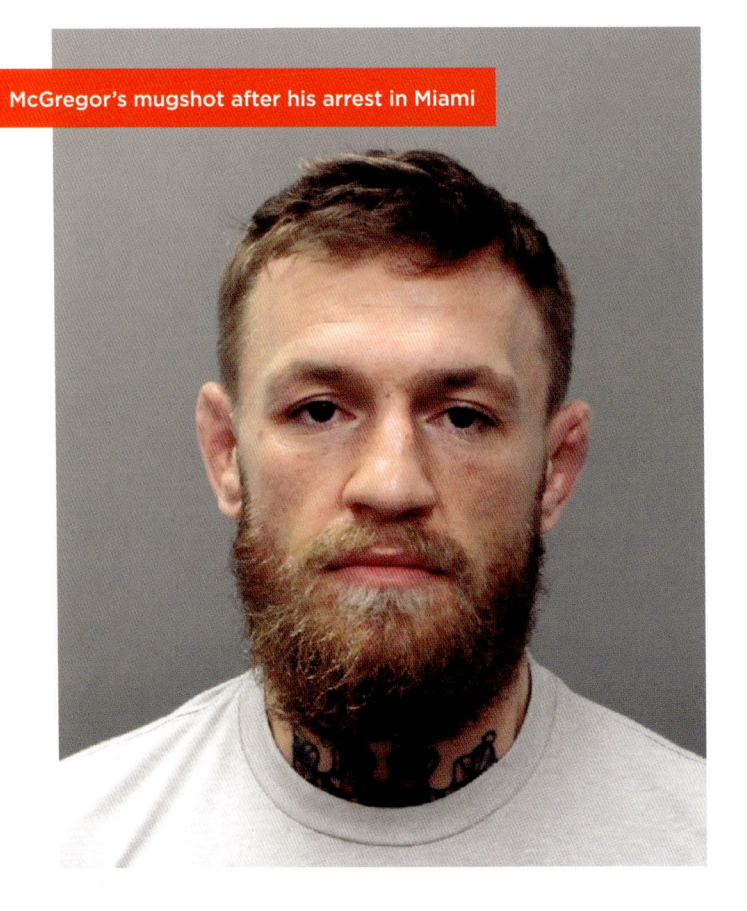

McGregor's troubles continued on April 6, when he allegedly punched an older man in a Dublin pub after the man refused to drink the fighter's whiskey brand. McGregor pleaded guilty, paid a fine, and compensated the victim financially. There were more accusations of criminal behavior against McGregor. The Irish superstar,

"MCGREGOR ANNOUNCED ON TWITTER ON JUNE 6, 2020, THAT HE WAS RETIRING YET AGAIN."

who once could do no wrong in MMA, was spending more time in court than in the Octagon. Could he turn his life around?

After nearly a year of retirement, McGregor returned to fighting on January 18, 2020, to defeat Donald "Cowboy" Cerrone in a welterweight fight at UFC 246 at the T-Mobile Arena in Las Vegas. McGregor won the fight via TKO just 40 seconds into the first round. This was another record win for McGregor, who became the first UFC fighter to win with knockouts in featherweight, lightweight, and welterweight bouts. However, this comeback was cut short when McGregor announced on Twitter on June 6, 2020, that he was retiring yet again: "Hey guys I've decided to retire from fighting. Thank you all for the amazing memories! What a ride it's been!"

This third retirement ended on January 24, 2021, when McGregor fought Dustin Poirier (whom he had fought in 2014) at UFC 257 in the Etihad Arena on Fight Island in Abu Dhabi, United Arab Emirates. McGregor lost the fight via TKO in the second round. Poirier's kicks to McGregor's calf forced McGregor to take a six-month medical leave. McGregor fought Poirier for a third time on July 10 at UFC 264 in Las Vegas. McGregor lost the fight in round one, after the ringside doctor stopped the brawl. McGregor had suffered a broken shin. Once again, fans wondered if McGregor's career was over. Could he come back again?

McGregor walks off a press conference.

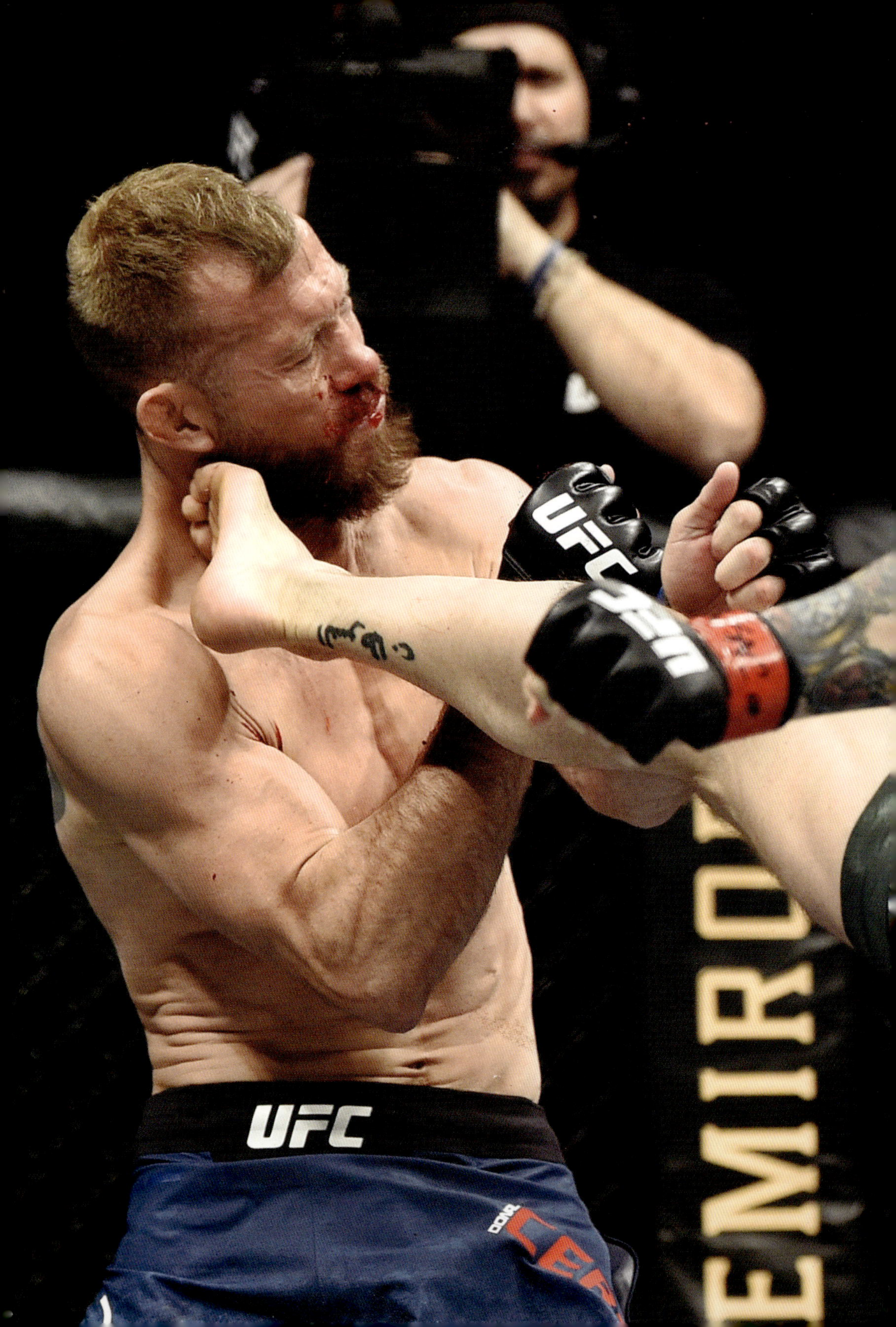
UFC
UFC

McGregor vs. Cerrone, 2020

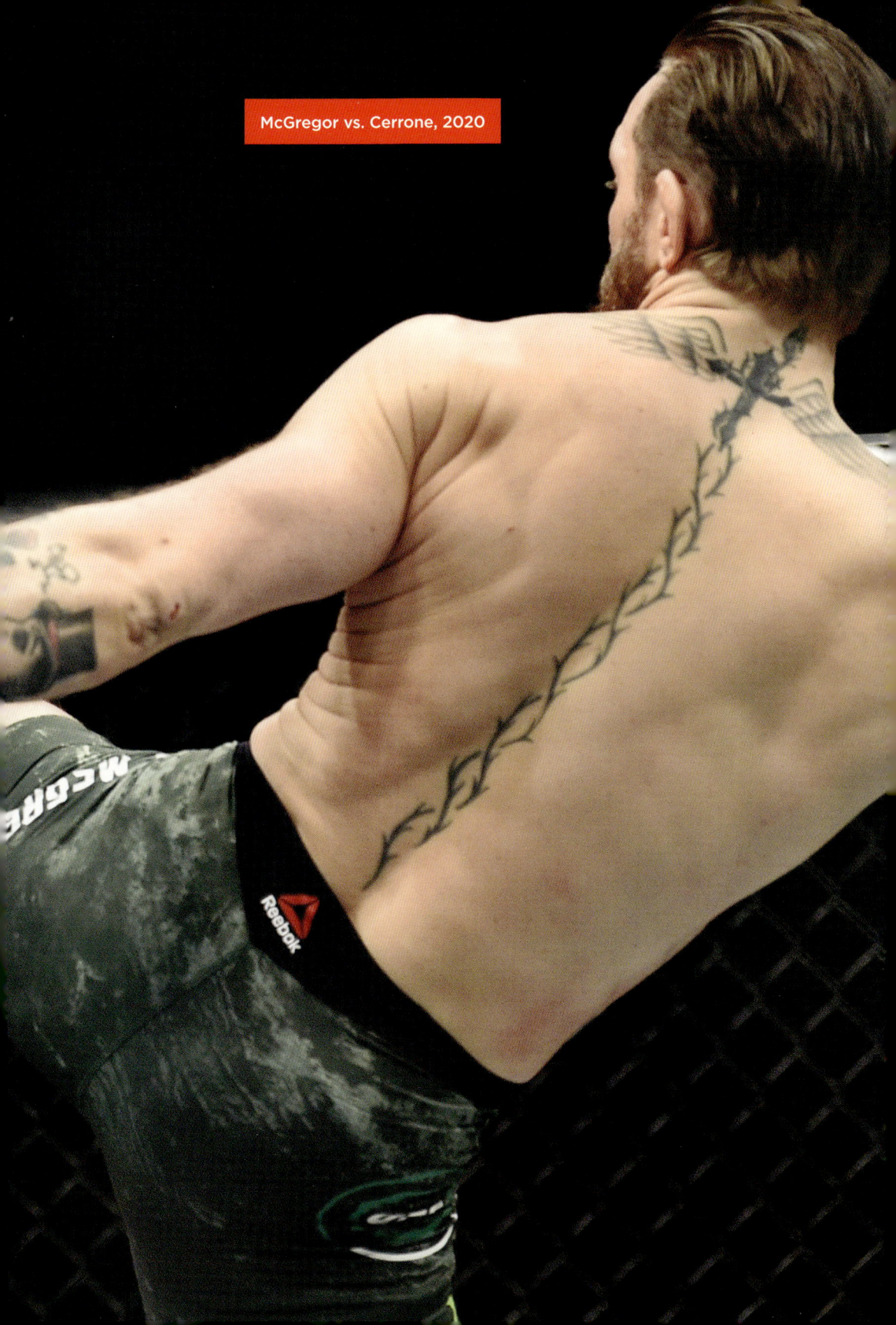

Cageside Press reported in February 2023 that McGregor would coach Season 31 of the reality show *The Ultimate Fighter* against Michael Chandler, and the pair would also fight later. (McGregor had coached on the show in 2015.) McGregor started the UFC's anti-doping program in October 2023, as six months of testing are required before fighting after a serious injury. The six-month timeline would have allowed McGregor and Chandler to fight at UFC 300 in April 2024, but McGregor announced that he would fight Chandler on June 29 instead. The June 29 date was also later quoted by *Fight Mag*.

Chandler confirmed to *MMA Fighting* he had hoped to fight McGregor in 2023, but it was not meant to be. White was asked on *The Pat McAfee Show* on February 7, 2024, if the McGregor–Chandler fight would ever happen. "Eventually," White replied. "Hopefully this year. There is no date. I'm hoping for the fall. [Hopefully] we get it done in the fall." Later that February, Chandler appeared on *WWE Raw* to ridicule McGregor: "I'm tired of waiting on Conor, so get his candy [expletive] back to the Octagon."

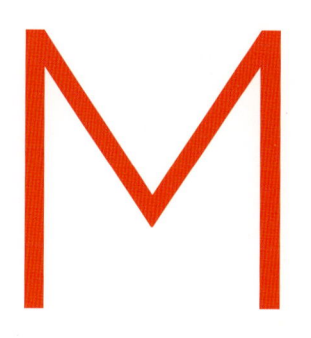

Meanwhile, McGregor has been promoting his new pub, Black Forged, and his beer brand, Forged Irish Stout, in Dublin. On April 27, 2024, McGregor also announced he had become a part owner of the Bare Knuckle Fighting Championship (BKFC) during BKFC Knucklemania 4 in Los Angeles.

McGregor has traveled far since watching MMA fights in Tom Egan's house. Who inspired him to reach for his dreams? He said on social media in 2023 that boxer Naseem Hamed "inspired me to become who I became." McGregor also said in 2023 that he "always wanted to meet Muhammad Ali. It would have been a dream of mine. He was a big inspiration for me, a hero." There is no doubt McGregor has joined his heroes as one of the all-time greats and is inspiring a new generation of future MMA fighters.

Conor McGregor reacts to his victory over Chad Mendes in the interim featherweight title fight at UFC 189 on July 11, 2015, in Las Vegas, Nevada.

Selected Bibliography

Conor M. and Samuel O. *Conor McGregor: Me You Never See-My Successful Career and The Journey So Far.* Legends Publication, 2021.

Faurote, Adrienne. *"UFC's Conor McGregor: From Small Town to Global Domination."* Haute Time, August, 18, 2016, https://www.hautetime.com/ufc-s-conor-mcgregor-from-small-town-to-global-domination/.

Gigney, George. *"The secret behind Conor McGregor's striking skills."* Boxing News, August 22, 2016, https://boxingnewsonline.net/the-secret-behind-conor-mcgregors-striking-skills/

Kavanagh, John. *Win or Learn: MMA, Conor McGregor & Me: A Trainer's Journey.* Penguin UK, 2018.

Lauletta, Tyler. *"How Conor McGregor went from Dublin plumber to the king of combat sports."* Business Insider, January, 21, 2021, https://www.businessinsider.com/conor-mcgregor-from-plumber-to-prize-fighter-2017-7#in-dublin-mcgregor-would-meet-his-now-.

Ott, Tim. *"Conor McGregor."* Biography, May 17, 2021, https://www.biography.com/athletes/conor-mcgregor.

Slack, Jack. *Notorious: The Biography of Conor McGregor.* John Blake, 2018.

Svelnis, Alexander. *Conor McGregor: Singleness of Purpose.* Self-published; Sold by Amazon.com Services LLC, 2018.

Glossary

anterior cruciate ligament (ACL) a ligament in the knee

featherweight in UFC, a fighter who weighs 136–145 pounds (61.7-65.8 kg)

guillotine a move used to choke an opponent and make them tap out in a fight. A fighter wraps his arm around his opponent's neck. The fighter then pulls the opponent's head down towards their chest to increase pressure on the neck.

lightweight in UFC, a fighter who weighs 146 to 155 pounds (66 to 70 kg)

Octagon the eight-sided raised platform surrounded by fencing that is used for UFC fights. The angles are wider than a square, preventing fighters from getting trapped.

orthodox stance a stance that places a fighter's left hand and left foot towards the front and the right hand (stronger side for most) farther back. This gives the fighter more time to speed up right hand punches.

pay-per-view (PPV) a private broadcast of an MMA fight that people can pay a one-time fee to watch on their TV

rear naked choke a chokehold applied from an opponent's back

southpaw stance a stance that places a fighter's right hand and right foot forward. This type of stance is often used by fighters who are left-handed, as it gives them more time to speed up a left blow.

technical knockout (TKO) when a referee calls an end to a fight because one of the fighters is no longer able to continue to defend themselves in a reasonable manner

underhook when an MMA fighter puts their hands under their opponent's arm to control the shoulder and upper body

uppercut when a fighter throws an upward punch to hit their opponent's chin or other areas on the head. An uppercut is mostly used when fighters are close together, to get full power behind the punch.

welterweight in UFC, a fighter who weighs 156 to 170 pounds (71 to 77 kg)

Websites

Irish folk hero: Conor McGregor goes from rags to riches with one brutal knockout
https://sports.yahoo.com/news/mma--a-star-is-born--irishman-conor-mcgregor-goes-from-rags-to-riches-with-one-brutal-knockout-022138398.html
This article tracks Conor McGregor's career from his early MMA fights in Europe to his signing with the UFC.

Like father, like son: Meet Tony McGregor, dad of 'The Notorious' UFC star Conor
https://www.independent.ie/style/celebrity/celebrity-news/like-father-like-son-meet-tony-mcgregor-dad-of-the-notorious-ufc-star-conor/34803633.html
Tony McGregor describes his famous son's upbringing in Ireland and how Conor became an MMA champion despite his parents' skepticism.

Outrageous Conor McGregor: His Irish Roots and an Improbable American Dream
https://bleacherreport.com/articles/2514254-outrageous-conor-mcgregor-his-irish-roots-and-an-improbable-american-dream
This overview tracks the career of Conor McGregor, from his teen years and boxing to adulthood and MMA superstardom.

True Stories of the Incredible, Unbelievable, Unstoppable Conor McGregor!
https://bleacherreport.com/articles/2727681-conor-mcgregor-stories-dublin-friends-coaches
Conor McGregor's coaches, friends, and fellow fighters recall his climb to UFC stardom and his preparation to fight boxer Floyd Mayweather.

Index

Aldo, Jose, 9, 10, 11, 37, 38, 41, 53
Ali, Muhammad, 74
Alvarez, Eddie, 50, 52, 53,
Anjos, Rafael dos, 43
Brandão, Diego, 33
Borg, Ray, 62
Brimage, Marcus, 31, 34
Byrd, Robert, 59
Cage Warriors, 25, 30
Cerrone, Donald "Cowboy," 67, 71
Chandler, Michael, 72, 73
Chiesa, Michael, 62
Crumlin Boxing Club, 16
Diaz, Nate, 43, 44, 45, 47, 48, 49
Dillon, Connor, 30
Dublin, Ireland, 15, 17, 21, 27, 33, 38, 58, 66, 73
Duffy, Joseph, 30
Egan, Tom, 18, 19, 21, 27, 51, 74
Hamed, Naseem, 74
Holloway, Max, 32
Kavanagh, John, 21, 25, 29, 49, 53, 54
Las Vegas, Nevada, 9, 13, 36, 37, 41, 43, 44, 49, 55, 58, 65, 67, 68, 75
Lobov, Artem, 57, 62
McGregor, Margaret, mother, 15, 16
McGregor, Tony, father, 15, 16, 17, 20, 25
Mayweather, Floyd, 43, 51, 55, 57, 58, 59, 61
Mendes, Chad, 38, 41, 75
Miller, Cole, 33
Morris, Gary, 25
Nurmagomedov, Khabib, 13, 61, 62, 64, 65
Ogle, Andy, 32
Poirier, Dustin, 2, 36, 39, 68
Sitenkov, Artemij, 27
Siver, Dennis, 36
Straight Blast Gym, 21
Sutcliffe, Phil, 16, 17
The Ultimate Fighter, 72
Tyson, Mike, 57
UFC 93, 27
UFC 178, 36
UFC 189, 37, 41, 75
UFC 194, 9, 41
UFC 196, 43
UFC 200, 48, 49
UFC 202, 48, 49
UFC 205, 50
UFC 223, 61
UFC 229, 13, 65
UFC 246, 5, 67
UFC 257, 68
UFC 264, 68
UFC 300, 72
UFC Fight Night 26, 32
UFC Fight Night 46, 33
UFC Fight Night 59, 36
White, Dana, 28, 30, 31, 38, 49, 61, 62, 65, 72, 73